A Whole Lotta Knock-Knock Jokes

A WHOLE LOTTA
KNOCK-KNOCK
JOKES

Squeaky-Clean Family Fun!

Mike and Heather Spohr

Illustrations by Dylan Goldberger

ROCKRIDGE
PRESS

Art Director: Eric Pratt
Art Producer: Sue Bischofberger
Editor: Erin Nelson
Production Manager: Riley Hoffman
Production Editor: Jenna Dutton

Illustrations © 2019 Dylan Goldberger • dylangoldberger.com

ISBN: Print 978-1-64152-928-0 | eBook 978-1-64152-929-7

KNOCK-KNOCK

Who's there?

We dedicate.

We dedicate who?

We dedicate this book to Annabel and James, our kids, whom we love very, very much!

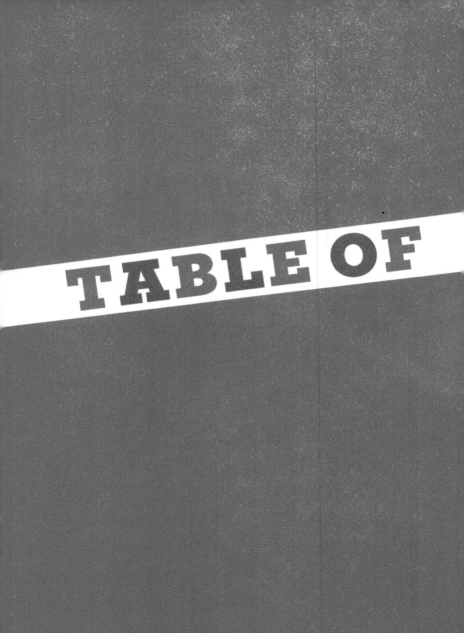

TABLE OF

CONTENTS

People have been telling knock-knock jokes for hundreds of years. In fact, William Shakespeare may have told the first knock-knock joke in his play Macbeth, all the way back in 1606!

Why do people love knock-knock jokes? Because they're funny! They're also fun to tell because they're meant to be said out loud, which means you get to perform them. The more fun you have performing the joke, the more people will laugh!

In addition to jokes, this book has a master riddle for you to solve:

A doctor and a teacher love the same girl. The doctor gave her a rose every day, but the teacher gave her an apple every day. Why did the teacher give her an apple every day?

Hunt for pages that have a over the page number. On these pages, jot down the words that appear in red. Put all of these words together and you'll have the answer to the riddle!

Ready to get started?

Knock, knock yourself out!

CHAPTER 1
ANIMALS

Knock, knock.
Who's there?
Hawk.
Hawk who?
**Hawk to the hand, because
the ears aren't listening.**

Knock, knock.
Who's there?
Iguana.
Iguana who?
Iguana play Fortnite.
Do you?

Knock, knock.
Who's there?
Baby shark.
Baby shark who?
**Baby shark, who who
who who who who
Baby shark, who who
who who who who
Baby shark, who who
who who who who
Baby shark!**

Knock, knock.
Who's there?
Cheetah.
Cheetah who?
**Cheetahs never win and
winners never cheat.**

Knock, knock.
Who's there?
Weasel.
Weasel who?
**Weasel Girl Scout
Cookies. Would you like
to buy some?**

Knock, knock.
Who's there?
Minnow.
Minnow who?
**Let minnow what
you think.**

Knock, knock.
Who's there?
Hedgehog.
Hedgehog who?
**Hedgehog Harry.
You were hoping it was
Sonic the Hedgehog,
weren't you?**

Knock, knock.
Who's there?
Pig.
Pig who?
**Pig up your clothes!
Your room is a mess.**

Knock, knock.
Who's there?
Parrot.
Parrot who?
**Parrot who? Parrot who?
Parrot who?**

Knock, knock.
Who's there?
Whale.
Whale who?
**Whale, whale, whale,
what have we here?**

Knock, knock.
Who's there?
Owl.
Owl who?
Owl by myself and lonely.

Knock, knock.
Who's there?
Giraffe.
Giraffe who?
**Giraffe-ing at me,
aren't you?**

Knock, knock.
Who's there?
Koala.
Koala who?
**Koala me
whatever you like.**

Knock, knock.
Who's there?
Otter.
Otter who?
**Let's get otter here,
we're running late!**

Knock, knock.
Who's there?
Alpaca.
Alpaca who?
**Alpaca suitcase
because I want to
take a trip!**

Knock, knock.
Who's there?
Lion.
Lion who?
**Quit lion, you
know who I am.**

Knock, knock.
Who's there?
Toad.
Toad who?
**Toad-ally awesome,
that's what I am!**

Knock, knock.
Who's there?
Ostrich.
Ostrich who?
Ostrich before I exercise.

Knock, knock.
Who's there?
Shellfish.
Shellfish who?
**It's shellfish to eat
all of the cake!**

Knock, knock.
Who's there?
Ewe.
Ewe who?
Ewe who, I'm here!

Knock, knock.
Who's there?
Bee.
Bee who?
**Bee-fore you ask, look
through the window.**

Knock, knock.
Who's there?
Macaw.
Macaw who?
**Macaw broke down in
South Boston.**

Knock, knock.
Who's there?
Pop star Terrier.
Pop star Terrier who?
Pop star Terrier Swift.

Knock, knock.
Who's there?
Bird.
Bird who?
**Bird any good
jokes lately?**

Knock, knock.
Who's there?
Dolphin.
Dolphin who?
**My dad goes dolphin
on the weekends.**

Knock, knock.
Who's there?
Gopher.
Gopher who?
Gopher it. You can do it!

Knock, knock.
Who's there?
Pigeon.
Pigeon who?
Pigeon nothing but fastballs.

Knock, knock.
Who's there?
Panda.
Panda who?
**Panda nail with
the hammer.**

Knock, knock.
Who's there?
Panther.
Panther who?
Panther the door!

Knock, knock.
Who's there?
Manatee.
Manatee who?
Oh, the hu-manatee!

Knock, knock.
Who's there?
Elephant.
Elephant who?
**It's irr-elephant who
I am, just let me in!**

Knock, knock.
Who's there?
Hare.
Hare who?
**Hare today,
gone tomorrow.**

Knock, knock!
Who's there?
Roach.
Roach who?
**Roach you a letter to tell
you I was coming.**

Knock, knock.
Who's there?
Weevil.
Weevil who?
**Weevil, weevil,
rock you.**

Knock, knock.
Who's there?
Goat.
Goat who?
**Goat to the door to see
who's knocking.**

Knock, knock.
Who's there?
Cows go.
Cows go who?
No, Cows go, "Moo!"

Knock knock.
Who's there?
Chicken.
Chicken who?
You, if you don't answer the door!

Knock, knock.
Who's there?
Goldfish.
Goldfish who?
Enough with the questions. Put me back in the bowl!

Knock, knock.
Who's there?
Gallop.
Gallop who?
Gallop in a tree. Get her down!

Knock, knock.
Who's there?
Rabbit.
Rabbit who?
Rabbit up, I'll take it.

Knock, knock.
Who's there?
Meow.
Meow who?
Meow-ie hurts! Got a Band-Aid?

Knock, knock.
Who's there?
Moose.
Moose who?
Moose gonna let me in?

Knock, knock.
Who's there?
Snake.
Snake who?
Snake your time, why don't you?

Knock, knock.
Who's there?
Squirrel.
Squirrel who?
Squirrel-y bird gets the worm.

Knock, knock.
Who's there?
Buffalo.
Buffalo who?
Buffalo the leader!

Knock, knock.
Who's there?
Some bunny.
Some bunny who?
**Some bunny who is tired
of all of these questions.**

Knock, knock.
Who's there?
Flea.
Flea who?
**Flea little pigs who
can't reach the doorbell.**

Knock, knock.
Who's there?
Monkey.
Monkey who?
Monkey see, monkey do.

Knock, knock.
Who's there?
Rhino.
Rhino who?
**Rhino every knock-knock
joke there is!**

Knock, knock.
Who's there?
Pooch.
Pooch who?
**Pooch your arms out for
an enormous hug.**

Knock, knock.
Who's there?
Puma.
Puma who?
I just puma pants!

Knock, knock.
Who's there?
Goose.
Goose who?
Goose who it is.

Knock, knock.
Who's there?
Senior.
Senior who?
**Senior dog digging in
the trash yesterday.**

Knock, knock.
Who's there?
Baby owl.
Baby owl who?
**Baby owl see you later,
maybe I won't.**

Knock, knock.
Who's there?
Fido.
Fido who?
**Fido I have to
wait outside?**

Knock, knock.
Who's there?
Gorilla.
Gorilla who?
**Gorilla hamburger
for me, please.**

Knock, knock!
Who's there?
Labrador.
Labrador who?
**Labrador won't
open itself.**

Knock, knock.
Who's there?
Kitten.
Kitten who?
**Stop kitten around
and be serious!**

Knock, knock.
Who's there?
Cobra.
Cobra who?
Cobra-sh your teeth!

Knock, knock.
Who's there?
Toucan.
Toucan who?
**Toucan play at
this game.**

Knock, knock.
Who's there?
Chimp.
Chimp who?
**Chimp-oo goes in
your hair!**

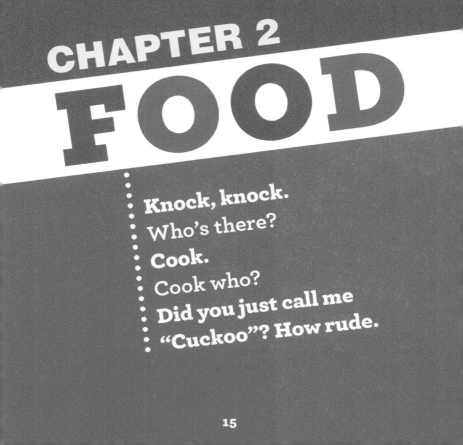

CHAPTER 2
FOOD

Knock, knock.
Who's there?
Cook.
Cook who?
Did you just call me
"Cuckoo"? How rude.

Knock, knock.
Who's there?
Beets.
Beets who?
Beets me.

Knock, knock.
Who's there?
Omelet.
Omelet who?
Omelet you know once you open the door.

Knock, knock.
Who's there?
Waiter.
Waiter who?
Waiter minute and I'll bring your quesadilla.

Knock, knock.
Who's there?
Berry waffle.
Berry waffle who?
Berry waffle weather out here, let me in!

Knock, knock.
Who's there?
Bread.
Bread who?
Bread any good books lately?

Knock, knock.
Who's there?
Donut.
Donut who?
Donut make you mad when you're covered in glaze?

Knock, knock.
Who's there?
It's sushi.
It's sushi who?
It's sushi wants you to come out and play!

Knock, knock.
Who's there?
Lettuce.
Lettuce who?
Lettuce in and you'll see.

Knock, knock.
Who's there?
Arthur.
Arthur who?
Arthur any cookies in your lunchbox you want to trade?

Knock, knock.
Who's there?
Berry.
Berry who?
**The Tooth Berry left
me five dollars.**

Knock, knock.
Who's there?
Ice cream.
Ice cream who?
**Ice cream if you
won't let me in.**

Knock, knock.
Who's there?
Apple.
Apple who?
**Apple your weight
around here, would you?**

Knock, knock.
Who's there?
Figs.
Figs who?
Figs your doorbell.

Knock, knock.
Who's there?
Butter.
Butter who?
**It's butter if
you don't know.**

Knock, knock.
Who's there?
Jalapeño.
Jalapeño who?
**Don't make me get
jalapeño business.**

Knock, knock.
Who's there?
Aida.
Aida who?
**Aida bunch of candy.
Don't tell my mom!**

Knock, knock.
Who's there?
Chow mein.
Chow mein who?
**Chow mein-y people
are you waiting for?**

Knock, knock.
Who's there?
Naan.
Naan who?
Naan of your business.

Knock, knock.
Who's there?
Halibut.
Halibut who?
Halibut we go to a movie?

Knock, knock.
Who's there?
Bean.
Bean who?
**Haven't you bean
paying attention?**

Knock, knock.
Who's there?
Barbie.
Barbie who?
**Barbie-cued some
burgers by the pool.**

Knock, knock.
Who's there?
Brie.
Brie who?
**Brie me some food
please, I'm starving!**

Knock, knock.
Who's there?
Peas.
Peas who?
**Peas let me in,
I wanna hang out.**

Knock, knock.
Who's there?
Poutine.
Poutine who?
**Poutine brown
gravy atop fries
and cheese curds!**

Knock, knock.
Who's there?
Abraham.
Abraham who?
**Abraham and cheese
sandwich, please.**

Knock, knock.
Who's there?
Asparagus.
Asparagus who?
**Asparagus your
excuses, okay?**

Knock, knock.
Who's there?
Olive.
Olive who?
Olive you!

Knock, knock.
Who's there?
Honey.
Honey who?
Honey, I'm home!

Knock, knock.
Who's there?
Pad Thai.
Pad Thai who?
**Pad Thai you're wearing
isn't cute, Dad.**

Knock, knock.
Who's there?
Hummus.
Hummus who?
**Hummus is that
doggie in the window?**

Knock, knock.
Who's there?
Bacon.
Bacon who?
Bacon me wait, are you?

Knock, knock.
Who's there?
Pudding.
Pudding who?
**Pudding this dessert
in my belly.**

Knock, knock.
Who's there?
Mushroom.
Mushroom who?
**Is there mushroom
in there?**

Knock, knock.
Who's there?
Orange.
Orange who?
**Orange you glad
to see me?**

Knock, knock.
Who's there?
Ben and Anna.
Ben and Anna who?
**Ben and Anna split
with whipped cream
and nuts, please!**

Knock, knock.
Who's there?
Dishes.
Dishes who?
Dishes me, who are you?

Knock, knock.
Who's there?
Carrot.
Carrot who?
**Do you carrot
all about me?**

Knock, Knock.
Who's there?
Cheesesteak.
Cheesesteak who?
**Cheesesteak caution
when crossing the street.**

Knock, knock.
Who's there?
Cantaloupe.
Cantaloupe who?
**She cantaloupe with
you, she's married!**

Knock, knock.
Who's there?
Sherwood.
Sherwood who?
**Sherwood like
a juice box.**

Knock, knock.
Who's there?
Juicy.
Juicy who?
Juicy what I see?

Knock, knock.
Who's there?
Moosh.
Moosh who?
Pork!

Knock, knock.
Who's there?
Pho.
Pho who?
**Pho-get it, I'm going
somewhere else.**

Knock, knock.
Who's there?
Turnip.
Turnip who?
**Turnip the movie,
I can't hear it!**

Knock, knock.
Who's there?
Phillip.
Phillip who?
**Phillip my plate with
chicken nuggets.**

Knock, knock.
Who's there?
Mayo.
Mayo who?
**Mayo dreams
all come true.**

(Said to a woman)
Knock, knock.
Who's there?
Mammal.
Mammal who?
No, mammal not tell you my last name.

Knock, knock.
Who's there?
Pasta.
Pasta who?
Pasta test and you'll get an "A"!

Knock, knock.
Who's there?
Cash.
Cash who?
No thanks, do you have any walnuts?

Knock, knock!
Who's there?
Diana.
Diana who?
Diana thirst, can I please have some water?!

Knock, knock.
Who's there?
Cold soda.
Cold soda who?
It's cold soda door should be closed.

Knock, knock.
Who's there?
Egg.
Egg who?
Egg-cellent, you're home. Let's go play!

Knock, knock.
Who's there?
Candy.
Candy who?
Candy person who blocked my driveway please move their car?

Knock, knock.
Who's there?
Relish.
Relish who?
Relish today, let's ketchup tomorrow.

Knock, knock.
Who's there?
Esme.
Esme who?
Esme tea ready yet?

Knock, knock.
Who's there?
Honeydew.
Honeydew who?
**Honeydew you want to
go to the movies tonight?**

Knock, knock.
Who's there?
Pecan.
Pecan who?
**Pecan somebody
your own size!**

Knock, knock.
Who's there?
Cereal.
Cereal who?
**Cereal pleasure
to meet you.**

Knock, knock.
Who's there?
Wilma.
Wilma who?
**Wilma dinner be ready
soon? It smells great!**

Knock, knock.
Who's there?
Curry.
Curry who?
**Curry me into your
home, I hurt my back!**

CHAPTER 3
NAMES

Knock, knock.
Who's there?
Imani.
Imani who?
Imani horse.
Want to ride one, too?

Knock, knock.
Who's there?
Erin.
Erin who?
**Erin on the side
of caution.**

Knock, knock.
Who's there?
Wyatt.
Wyatt who?
**Wyatt taking you so long
to answer the door?**

Knock, knock.
Who's there?
Shelby.
Shelby who?
**Shelby comin' round
the mountain when
she comes.**

Knock, knock.
Who's there?
Juana.
Juana who?
**Juana come out
and play?**

Knock, knock.
Who's there?
Wayne.
Wayne who?
**Wayne is coming
down in buckets!**

Knock, knock.
Who's there?
Hannah.
Hannah who?
Hannah over the money!

Knock, knock.
Who's there?
Hayden.
Hayden who?
**Hayden seek is my
favorite game!**

Knock, knock.
Who's there?
Noah.
Noah who?
**Noah-body knows the
troubles I've seen.**

Knock, knock.
Who's there?
Avery.
Avery who?
Avery day
I'm hustlin'.

Knock, knock.
Who's there?
Leah.
Leah who?
Leah message and
I'll get back to you.

Knock, knock.
Who's there?
Dwayne.
Dwayne who?
Dwayne the bathtub,
it's overflowing.

Knock, knock.
Who's there?
Freddie.
Freddie who?
Freddie or not,
here I come!

Knock, knock.
Who's there?
Paul.
Paul who?
Paul harder,
the door is stuck!

Knock, knock.
Who's there?
Heidi.
Heidi who?
Heidi 'cided to
come over to play.

Knock, knock.
Who's there?
Linda.
Linda who?
Linda hand, I can't
do this all by myself!

Knock, knock.
Who's there?
Annie.
Annie who?
Annie-body home?

Knock, knock.
Who's there?
Rufus.
Rufus who?
**Rufus leaking and
I'm getting wet!**

Knock, knock.
Who's there?
Diego.
Diego who?
**Diego is my favorite
breakfast treat.**

Knock, knock.
Who's there?
Omar.
Omar who?
Omar goodness!
I'm locked out,
please let me in.

Knock, knock.
Who's there?
Tyson.
Tyson who?
Tyson of this on for size.

Knock, knock.
Who's there?
Raul.
Raul who?
Raul with the punches.

Knock, knock.
Who's there?
Yvonne.
Yvonne who?
Yvonne to be alone.

Knock, knock.
Who's there?
Tamara.
Tamara who?
Tamara there's no
school. Let's go
do something!

Knock, knock.
Who's there?
Zeke.
Zeke who?
Zeke and you shall find.

Knock, knock.
Who's there?
Mikey.
Mikey who?
Mikey isn't working and
the door is locked.

Knock, knock.
Who's there?
Brooklyn.
Brooklyn who?
Brooklyn the peephole
and you'll see.

Knock, knock.
Who's there?
Yoda.
Yoda who?
Yoda-Lay-Hee-Hoo!

Knock, knock.
Who's there?
Emma.
Emma who?
**Emma-rican Girl Dolls
are my favorite.**

Knock, knock.
Who's there?
Eva.
Eva who?
Happy Eva after.

Knock, knock.
Who's there?
Mason.
Mason who?
**Mason always shine
on your back.**

Knock, knock.
Who's there?
Amelia.
Amelia who?
**Amelia should eat
is breakfast.**

Knock, knock.
Who's there?
Mia.
Mia who?
Mi'and my shadow.

Knock, knock.
Who's there?
James.
James who?
James people play.

Knock, knock.
Who's there?
Alex.
Alex who?
Alex-splain later.

Knock, knock.
Who's there?
Michelle.
Michelle who?
Michelle has a crab in it.

Knock, knock.
Who's there?
Robin.
Robin who?
**Robin you! Hand
over your goods.**

Knock, knock.
Who's there?
Benjamin.
Benjamin who?
Benjamin to the radio!

Knock, knock.
Who's there?
Miss.
Miss who?
Miss-placed my key!

Knock, knock.
Who's there?
Isaac.
Isaac who?
**"Isaac your blood,"
said the vampire.**

Knock, knock.
Who's there?
Aliyah.
Aliyah who?
**Aliyah leftover pizza
in the fridge.**

Knock, knock.
Who's there?
Allie.
Allie who?
Allie want is to be let in!

Knock, knock.
Who's there?
Mateo.
Mateo who?
Mateo is as old as time.

Knock, knock.
Who's there?
Nathan.
Nathan who?
Nathan to see here.

Knock, knock.
Who's there?
Sarah.
Sarah who?
Sarah problem here?

Knock, knock.
Who's there?
Ebony.
Ebony who?
**Ebony just hopped
across the road! So cute!**

Knock, knock.
Who's there?
Jamal.
Jamal who?
**Jamal up in
your business.**

Knock, knock.
Who's there?
Isabelle.
Isabelle who?
**Isabelle not working?
I had to knock.**

Knock, knock.
Who's there?
José.
José who?
**José can you see, by the
dawn's early light?**

Knock, knock.
Who's there?
Gus.
Gus who?
**That's what you're
supposed to do!**

Knock, knock.
Who's there?
Wanda.
Wanda who?
**Wanda come out and
play with me?**

Knock, knock.
Who's there?
Matthew!
Matthew who?
**Matthew lace has come
untied. Can you tie it
for me, please?**

Knock, knock.
Who's there?
Candice.
Candice who?
Candice door open?

Knock, knock.
Who's there?
Chester.
Chester who?
Chester minute, I think I'm at the wrong house!

Knock, knock.
Who's there?
Maria?
Maria who?
I'll Maria if you get down on one knee and propose!

Knock, knock.
Who's there?
Annabel.
Annabel who?
Annabel would be helpful, so I don't have to knock.

Knock, knock.
Who's there?
Carl.
Carl who?
Carl get you there quicker than walking.

Knock, knock.
Who's there?
Brent.
Brent who?
Don't get Brent out of shape.

Knock, knock.
Who's there?
Keira.
Keira who?
Keira my new song on the radio!

Knock, knock.
Who's there?
Howard.
Howard who?
Howard I know?

CHAPTER 4
NATURE

Knock, knock.
Who's there?
Garden.
Garden who?
Garden the treasure, a robber keeps trying to steal it.

Knock, knock.
Who's there?
Hurricane.
Hurricane who?
**Hurricane you bring
me an umbrella?**

Knock, knock.
Who's there?
Morning dew.
Morning dew who?
**Morning, dew you want
to go out for breakfast?**

Knock, knock.
Who's there?
Leaf.
Leaf who?
Leaf me alone!

Knock, knock.
Who's there?
Water.
Water who?
**Water you doing?
Let me in!**

Knock, knock.
Who's there?
Daisy.
Daisy who?
**Daisy me rollin',
they hatin'.**

Knock, knock.
Who's there?
Beehive.
Beehive who?
**Beehive yourself or
you'll get into trouble.**

Knock, knock.
Who's there?
Counting mountain.
Counting mountain who?
**Counting moun-ten,
eleven, twelve . . .**

Knock, knock.
Who's there?
Snow.
Snow who?
**Snow business like
show business.**

Knock, knock.
Who's there?
Ant.
Ant who?
**Ant-chovies on pizza
are gross. Yuck!**

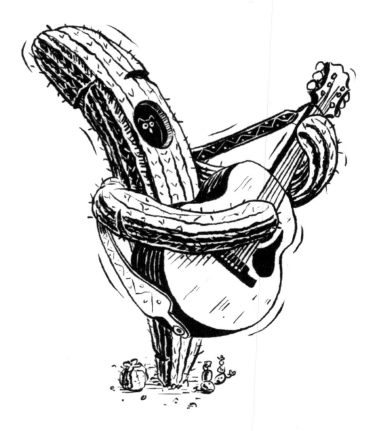

Knock, knock.
Who's there?
Cactus.
Cactus who?
Cactus makes perfect.

Knock, knock.
Who's there?
Theresa.
Theresa who?
**Theresa green
until the fall.**

Knock, knock.
Who's there?
Pasture.
Pasture who?
Pasture bedtime, isn't it?

Knock, knock.
Who's there?
Forest.
Forest who?
**Forest my
favorite number.**

Knock, knock.
Who's there?
Mist.
Mist who?
**Mister mailman,
you forgot a letter!**

Knock, knock.
Who's there?
Island.
Island who?
**Island at 4:00 p.m.
Can you pick me up?**

Knock, knock.
Who's there?
High tide.
High tide who?
**High tide calling,
but no one answered.**

Knock, knock.
Who's there?
Tulips.
Tulips who?
**Tulips, one nose,
two eyes!**

Knock, knock.
Who's there?
Sleet.
Sleet who?
Sl'eet, I'm starving.

Knock, knock.
Who's there?
Grass.
Grass who?
Grass me again later.

Knock, knock.
Who's there?
Ladybug.
Ladybug who?
**Ladybug someone
else for a while.**

Knock, knock.
Who's there?
Dessert.
Dessert who?
**Dessert is ready, it's
apple pie and ice cream!**

Knock, knock.
Who's there?
Larva.
Larva who?
I larva you, too.

Knock, knock.
Who's there?
Prairie.
Prairie who?
Prairie me, my love?

Knock, knock.
Who's there?
Hiking.
Hiking who?
Hiking, I bow before you!

Knock, knock.
Who's there?
Bertha.
Bertha who?
**Bertha quake just
shook my house!**

Knock, knock.
Who's there?
Flower.
Flower who?
Flower you feeling?

Knock, knock.
Who's there?
Stream.
Stream who?
**Stream a little
dream of me.**

Knock, knock.
Who's there?
Rainforest.
Rainforest who?
Rainforest, run!

Knock, knock.
Who's there?
Grassy.
Grassy who?
**Feeling grassy after
that burger.**

Knock, knock.
Who's there?
Canyon.
Canyon who?
Canyon goes boom!

Knock, knock.
Who's there?
Dandelion.
Dandelion who?
**Dandelion keeps getting
out of his cage!**

Knock, knock.
Who's there?
Quicksand.
Quicksand who?
**Quicksand for the
national anthem!**

Knock, knock.
Who's there?
Waterfall.
Waterfall who?
**Waterfall these
people doing here?**

Knock, knock.
Who's there?
Cloudy.
Cloudy who?
Cloudy, partner!
Yee-haw!

Knock, knock.
Who's there?
Lake.
Lake who?
I lake you.

Knock, knock.
Who's there?
Drought.
Drought who?
**Drought of water
in the kitchen.**

Knock, knock.
Who's there?
Valley.
Valley who?
**Valley-ball is my
favorite sport.**

Knock, knock.
Who's there?
Icicle.
Icicle who?
Icicl-est kid in my class.

Knock, knock.
Who's there?
Stormy.
Stormy who?
**Stormy treasure
below deck, arrrgh!**

Knock, knock.
Who's there?
Butterfly.
Butterfly who?
**Butterfly if you want
to visit Australia.**

Knock, knock.
Who's there?
Boulder.
Boulder who?
Boulder and wiser.

Knock, knock.
Who's there?
Weed.
Weed who?
**Extra! Extra!
Weed all about it!**

Knock, knock.
Who's there?
Brook.
Brook who?
**Brook my arm
falling from a tree!**

Knock, knock.
Who's there?
Cliff.
Cliff who?
**Cliff you go too far,
you'll fall off.**

Knock, knock.
Who's there?
Thorn.
Thorn who?
**Thor'n Spider-Man are
my favorite Avengers.**

Knock, knock.
Who's there?
Mighty worm.
Mighty worm who?
**Mighty worm weather
we're having.**

Knock, knock.
Who's there?
Branch.
Branch who?
**Branch dressing
is delicious.**

Knock, knock.
Who's there?
Bumblebee.
Bumblebee who?
**Bumblebee cold if
your pants fall down.**

Knock, knock.
Who's there?
Lily pad.
Lily pad who?
**Lily pad weather out
here, open up!**

Knock, knock.
Who's there?
Sand dune.
Sand dune who?
**Sand dune the
next patient!**

Knock, knock.
Who's there?
Kelp.
Kelp who?
Kelp me, I can't swim!

Knock, knock.
Who's there?
Shrub.
Shrub who?
**Shrub the lamp and
get three wishes!**

Knock, knock.
Who's there?
Plants.
Plants who?
**Plants are made
to be broken.**

Knock, knock.
Who's there?
Breeze.
Breeze who?
**Breeze trees sure
are pretty.**

Knock, knock.
Who's there?
Willow.
Willow who?
**Willow you if you
buy me lunch.**

Knock, knock.
Who's there?
Moss.
Moss who?
Moss at home with Pa.

Knock, knock.
Who's there?
Arctic.
Arctic who?
**Arctics going to
bite me in the woods?**

Knock, knock.
Who's there?
Termite.
Termite who?
Termite is the night.

Knock, knock!
Who's there?
Thunder.
Thunder who?
**Thunder wear is dirty,
throw 'em in the wash!**

CHAPTER 5
PLACES

Knock, knock.
Who's there?
Canada.
Canada who?
Canada and cat be friends?

Knock, knock.
Who's there?
Sweden.
Sweden who?
Sweden the cake!
It tastes awful!

Knock, knock.
Who's there?
Alaska.
Alaska who?
Alaska to open the
door one last time.

Knock, knock.
Who's there?
France.
France who?
France-y seeing
you here.

Knock, knock.
Who's there?
Shanghai.
Shanghai who?
**Shanghai to you
and your family.**

Knock, knock.
Who's there?
Brazil.
Brazil who?
**Brazillionaire out here!
Want some money?**

Knock, knock.
Who's there?
Delaware.
Delaware who?
**Delaware your New
Jersey to the game
tomorrow.**

Knock, knock.
Who's there?
Utah.
Utah who?
Utah-king to me?

Knock, knock.
Who's there?
Tibet.
Tibet who?
Early Tibet, early to rise.

Knock, knock.
Who's there?
Europe.
Europe who?
**That's a rude way to
greet a guest!**

Knock, knock.
Who's there?
Kenya.
Kenya who?
**Kenya let me in?
It's pouring out here.**

Knock, knock.
Who's there?
Arizona.
Arizona who?
**Arizona room enough
for one of us. Duel!**

Knock, knock.
Who's there?
Perth.
Perth who?
Perth your lips together to whistle.

Knock, knock.
Who's there?
Israel.
Israel who?
Israel nice to meet you!

Knock, knock.
Who's there?
Iraq.
Iraq who?
Iraq 'n' roll!

Knock, knock.
Who's there?
Singapore.
Singapore who?
Singapore song and I'll cover my ears.

Knock, knock.
Who's there?
Norway.
Norway who?
Norway am I leaving before you open this door.

Knock, knock.
Who's there?
Ida.
Ida who?
No, it's not Ida-who, it's Idaho!

Knock, knock.
Who's there?
Bolivia.
Bolivia who?
Bolivia not, here I am!

Knock, knock.
Who's there?
Yukon.
Yukon who?
Yukon let me in and find out.

Knock, knock.
Who's there?
Cow farm.
Cow farm who?
Cow far'm I from the city?

Knock, knock.
Who's there?
Circus.
Circus who?
**Circus your wife.
I just pronounced
you married.**

Knock, knock.
Who's there?
Juneau.
Juneau who?
**Juneau the
capital of Alaska?**

Knock, knock.
Who's there?
Ottawa.
Ottawa who?
**Ottawa know you're
telling the truth?**

Knock, knock.
Who's there?
Rome.
Rome who?
**Rome is where
the heart is.**

Knock, knock.
Who's there?
Iran.
Iran who?
**Iran all the way here to
see if you wanted to play!**

Knock, knock.
Who's there?
Russia.
Russia who?
**Russia to the door
and let me in.**

Knock, knock.
Who's there?
A mall.
A mall who?
A mall shook up!

Knock, knock.
Who's there?
Taipei.
Taipei who?
**Taipei 60 words a minute
on my computer.**

Knock, knock.
Who's there?
Italy.
Italy who?
Italy hot today.

Knock, knock.
Who's there?
Uruguay.
Uruguay who?
Uruguay your way and I'll go mine.

Knock, knock.
Who's there?
Venice.
Venice who?
Venice the party starting?

Knock, knock.
Who's there?
Hawaii.
Hawaii who?
I'm great, thanks! Hawaii you?

Knock, knock.
Who's there?
Arkansas.
Arkansas who?
Arkansas wood faster than you!

Knock, knock.
Who's there?
Armenia.
Armenia who?
Armenia every word I say.

Knock, knock.
Who's there?
Missouri.
Missouri who?
Missouri loves company.

Knock, knock.
Who's there?
Little Rock.
Little Rock who?
Little Rock 'n' roll will get this party started!

Knock, knock.
Who's there?
Havana.
Havana who?
Havana a wonderful time, wish you were here!

Knock, knock.
Who's there?
Vampire.
Vampire who?
**Vampire State Building is one
of the tallest in New York.**

Knock, knock.
Who's there?
Tennessee.
Tennessee who?
Tennis, see? They're playing across the street.

Knock, knock.
Who's there?
Jamaica.
Jamaica who?
Jamaica delicious jerk chicken.

Knock, knock.
Who's there?
Mumbai.
Mumbai who?
Mumbai some cookies at the store!

Knock, knock.
Who's there?
Iowa.
Iowa who?
Iowa lot of money to the bank.

Knock, knock.
Who's there?
Ore.
Ore who?
Ore.
Ore who?!
It's Oregon.

Knock, knock.
Who's there?
Avenue.
Avenue who?
Avenue heard this joke before?

Knock, knock.
Who's there?
Cairo.
Cairo who?
**Cairo the boat
gently down the stream.**

Knock, knock.
Who's there?
Moscow.
Moscow who?
**Moscow has better milk
than Pa's cow!**

Knock, knock.
Who's there?
Charleston.
Charleston who?
**Charleston-ight is my
birthday party!**

Knock, knock.
Who's there?
Town.
Town who?
**Town that frown
upside down.**

Knock, knock.
Who's there?
Jupiter.
Jupiter who?
Jupiter toys away?

Knock, knock.
Who's there?
Dish.
Dish who?
Dish is a nice place.

Knock, knock.
Who's there?
Tokyo.
Tokyo who?
**Tokyo long enough to
answer the door.**

Knock, knock.
Who's there?
Sudan.
Sudan who?
**Put your Sudan so we
can go to the pool!**

Knock, knock.
Who's there?
Cinema.
Cinema who?
**Cinema rolls are my
favorite treat to eat.**

Knock, knock.
Who's there?
Austin.
Austin who?
Austin la vista, baby!

Knock, knock.
Who's there?
Maine.
Maine who?
**Maine-tain your
distance, I'm sick!**

Knock, knock.
Who's there?
Germany.
Germany who?
Germany fish in the sea.

Knock, knock.
Who's there?
Washington.
Washington who?
**Washingtons of clothes,
will you help me fold?**

Knock, knock.
Who's there?
Hollywood.
Hollywood who?
**Hollywood not like this
joke, she's humorless.**

Knock, knock.
Who's there?
Nevada.
Nevada who?
**I bet you Nevada
friend like me!**

Knock, knock.
Who's there?
Czech.
Czech who?
**Czech yourself before you
wreck yourself!**

CHAPTER 6
SCHOOL
IS COOL

Knock, knock.
Who's there?
P.E.
P.E. who?
P.E.U., you stink!

Knock, knock.
Who's there?
School spirit.
School spirit who?
Whooohooo oohhhhhohhh
(ghost sound).

Knock, knock.
Who's there?
Pop quiz.
Pop quiz who?
**Oh, were you not
expecting me?**

Knock, knock.
Who's there?
Abe.
Abe who?
Abe-e, C, D, E, F, G . . .

Knock, knock.
Who's there?
Beth.
Beth who?
Beth of all, school's almost over.

Knock, knock.
Who's there?
Art.
Art who?
Art2-D2.

Knock, knock.
Who's there?
Grammar.
Grammar who?
Grammar and Grandpa!

Knock, knock.
Who's there?
George Washington.
George Washington who?
You don't know George Washington?

Knock, knock.
Who's there?
Colin.
Colin who?
Colin absent to school and go to the doctor, you're sick.

Knock, knock.
Who's there?
Spell.
Spell who?
W-H-O.

Knock, knock.
Who's there?
Math book.
Math book who?
Enough questions! I've got my own problems!

Knock, knock.
Who's there?
Thermos.
Thermos who?
Thermos be some mistake, I'm sure I answered that right!

$$O + W = 1$$
$$W = 1 - O$$
$$W = 1$$

Knock, knock.
Who's there?
Owl.
Owl who?
Owlgebra is a tough subject.

Knock, knock.
Who's there?
Division.
Division who?
Division test is hard if you close your eyes.

Knock, knock.
Who's there?
Double.
Double who?
W.

Knock, knock.
Who's there?
To.
To who?
To whom.

Knock, knock.
Who's there?
Calculator.
Calculator who?
I'll calculator on the phone.

Knock, knock.
Who's there?
Pie.
Pie who?
3.1416 . . .

Knock, knock.
Who's there?
Zeroes.
Zeroes who?
Zeroes as fast as she can, but the boat doesn't move.

Knock, knock.
Who's there?
Tennis.
Tennis who?
Tennis my favorite number!

Knock, knock.
Who's there?
Compass.
Compass who?
Compass this test and you'll go on to the next grade.

Knock, knock.
Who's there?
Bully.
Bully who?
**Bully-ve me, it's
better to be nice.**

Knock, knock.
Who's there?
Board.
Board who?
**Brown v. Board of
Education was an
important case!**

Knock, knock.
Who's there?
Canoe.
Canoe who?
**Canoe help me with my
science homework?**

Knock, knock.
Who's there?
Student.
Student who?
**Student-ed my mom's
car with his bike!**

Knock, knock.
Who's there?
Unit.
Unit who?
**Unit socks,
I knit scarves.**

Knock, knock.
Who's there?
Dozen.
Dozen who?
**Dozen-y one know what
time recess ends?**

Knock, knock.
Who's there?
Schnauzer.
Schnauzer who?
Schnauzer homework coming?

Knock, knock.
Who's there?
Elf.
Elf who?
Elf-abet!

Knock, knock.
Who's there?
Kindergarten.
Kindergarten who?
Kindergarten is where you plant your flowers!

Knock, knock.
Who's there?
Acid.
Acid who?
Acid sit down and be quiet!

Knock, knock.
Who's there?
Broken pencil.
Broken pencil who?
Never mind, there's no point to this joke.

Knock, knock.
Who's there?
Warrior.
Warrior who?
Warrior been? School started an hour ago.

Knock, knock.
Who's there?
Gladys.
Gladys who?
Gladys the weekend.

Knock, knock.
Who's there?
Adam.
Adam who?
Adam up . . . 1 + 1 = 2.

Knock, knock.
Who's there?
Anita.
Anita who?
Anita borrow a pencil!

Knock, knock.
Who's there?
Reading.
Reading who?
**Reading-dong,
the witch is dead!**

Knock, knock.
Who's there?
Rita.
Rita who?
**Rita book for your
book report.**

Knock, knock.
Who's there?
School bus.
School bus who?
**School bus be boring
if you want to skip!**

Knock, knock.
Who's there?
Choir.
Choir who?
**Choir all these kids
singing together?**

Knock, knock.
Who's there?
Matthew.
Matthew who?
**Matthew learn in the
third grade is hard!**

Knock, knock.
Who's there?
Ahmed.
Ahmed who?
**Ahmed a mistake;
give me an eraser.**

Knock, knock.
Who's there?
Pencil.
Pencil who?
**Pencil fall down if you
don't wear a belt.**

Knock, knock.
Who's there?
Sum.
Sum who?
**Sum-mer is a teacher's
favorite time of year.**

Knock, knock.
Who's there?
Harvey.
Harvey who?
**Harvey ever going to be
released for recess?**

Knock, knock.
Who's there?
Ruler.
Ruler who?
**Ruler of the kingdom,
let me in!**

Knock, knock.
Who's there?
Dewey.
Dewey who?
**Dewey really have to
take a test tomorrow?**

Knock, knock.
Who's there?
Chalk.
Chalk who?
**Chalk-olate milk at
school costs one dollar.**

Knock, knock.
Who's there?
Prince.
Prince who?
**Prince-pal is the ruler
of the school!**

Knock, knock.
Who's there?
Justin.
Justin who?
Justin time for school!

Knock, knock.
Who's there?
Campus.
Campus who?
**Campus where I go
every summer.**

Knock, knock.
Who's there?
Pen.
Pen who?
Pen is school out?

Knock, knock.
Who's there?
Paper.
Paper who?
**Let's paper view a
movie tonight!**

Knock, knock.
Who's there?
Teacher.
Teacher who?
**Iced tea-cher is a
tasty drink.**

Knock, knock.
Who's there?
Diploma.
Diploma who?
**Diploma is here
to fix the sink.**

Knock, knock.
Who's there?
Pizza.
Pizza who?
**Pizza new student
in my class.**

Knock, knock.
Who's there?
Science.
Science who?
Shhh, science is golden.

Knock, knock.
Who's there?
Desk.
Desk who?
**Desk the halls with
boughs of holly,
fa la la la la, la la la la.**

Knock, knock.
Who's there?
Peas.
Peas who?
**"Peas be quiet!"
says the librarian.**

Knock, knock.
Who's there?
Essay.
Essay who?
Essay anything!

BONUS JOKES

Knock, knock.

Who's there?

Felix.

Felix who?

Felix my ice cream cone one more time, I'll scream!

KNOCK, KNOCK.

Knock, knock.
Who's there?
Pikachu.
Pikachu who?
**Pikachu your window
and see for yourself!**

- - -

Knock, knock.
Who's there?
Donkey.
Donkey who?
Don Quixote!

- - -

Knock, knock.
Who's there?
You know.
You know who?
Exactly.

- - -

Knock, knock.
Who's there?
Odor.
Odor who?
**Odor a little
deodorant, will ya?**

Knock, knock.
Who's there?
Suspense.
Suspense who?
I'll tell you tomorrow.

- - -

Knock, knock.
Who's there?
Says.
Says who?
Says me, that's who!

- - -

Knock, knock.
Who's there?
Repeat.
Repeat who?
**Who who who
who who . . .**

- - -

Knock, knock.
Who's there?
Adore.
Adore who?
**Adore is between us,
open up!**

Knock, knock.
Who's there?
Stopwatch.
Stopwatch who?
**Stopwatch you're
doing right now!**

Knock, knock.
Who's there?
Doctor.
Doctor who?
No, Doctor Strange!

**Will you remember
me in six days?**
Yes.
**Will you remember
me in six months?**
Yes.
**Will you remember
me in six years?**
Yes.
Knock, knock.
Who's there?
**YOU DON'T
REMEMBER ME?!**

Knock, knock.
Who's there?
Police.
Police who?
**Police let us in, it's
raining out here.**

Knock, knock.
Who's there?
Razor.
Razor who?
**Razor hands,
this is a stickup!**

Knock, knock.
Who's there?
Freeze.
Freeze who?
**Fr'eeze a jolly good
fellow, fr'eeze a jolly
good fellow . . .**

Knock, knock.
Who's there?
Lena.
Lena who?
**Lena little closer and
see for yourself.**

Knock, knock.
Who's there?
Amish.
Amish who?
Aw, Amish you, too.

Knock, knock.
Who's there?
Sorry.
Sorry who?
**Sorry, I'm at the
wrong house.**

Knock, knock.
Who's there?
Armageddon.
Armageddon who?
**Armageddon tired of
doing all this knocking!**

Knock, knock.
Who's there?
Radio.
Radio who?
Radio not, here I come!

**Why did the police go to
the baseball stadium?**
Because someone
stole second base.

**Why is England the
wettest country?**
Because the queen
has reigned for more
than 60 years.

**Why didn't the sun
go to college?**
Because it already has
27 million degrees.

**Where was the
Declaration of
Independence signed?**
At the bottom.

**Why should you never
date an apostrophe?**
They're too possessive.

**What did the hungry
clock do?**
Went back for seconds.

What does a shark eat with peanut butter?
A jellyfish.

What do you do when a fish sings flat?
Tuna fish.

What is an astronaut's favorite key on the keyboard?
The space bar.

Why didn't the guy get hurt when he was hit in the head with a can of soda?
It was a soft drink.

What do you give an injured lemon?
Lemonade.

Why aren't teddy bears ever hungry?
They're always stuffed.

**What do you call
it when a dinosaur
crashes his car?**
A Tyrannosaurus wreck.

**What do you call
a dinosaur with a
large vocabulary?**
A thesaurus.

**Why did Grandma sit in a rocking
chair with roller skates on?**
She wanted to rock 'n' roll.

Why did the chicken cross the playground?
To get to the other slide.

Why did the banana visit the doctor?
He wasn't peeling well.

Why did the hot dog wear a sweater?
It was a chili dog.

What dog always comes in first in races?
A weiner dog.

Why did the bucket go to the nurse's office?
It had a pail face.

What do you call a musical insect?
A humbug.

What is a skeleton's favorite instrument?
The trombone.

What do you call a lizard that performs hip hop?
A rap-tile.

What's a tornado's favorite song to dance to?
The Twist.

What did the calculator say to the student?
You can count on me!

Why did the ghost make the cheerleading squad?
They needed team spirit.

Which word in the dictionary is spelled incorrectly?
Incorrectly.

Why was the broom late for school?
It overswept.

What did the thief get when he stole a calendar?
Twelve months.

**What subject is a
witch good at?**
Spelling.

**What do you call a
bear with no teeth?**
A gummy bear.

**Why couldn't the
sailors play cards?**
They kept standing
on the deck.

**How does a scientist
fix her bad breath?**
With experi-mints.

**What do you call
a magical dog?**
A Labracadabrador.

**What do lawyers
wear when they go
to the courthouse?**
Lawsuits.

**Why do birds fly away
for the winter?**
It's too far to walk.

**Did you hear the joke
about the roof?**
Never mind, it's
over your head.

**What time do
ducks wake up?**
At the quack of dawn.

**Why should dogs
never be in charge
of the remote?**
They keep hitting paws.

**Why was the weightlifter
always frustrated?**
He worked with
dumbbells.

RIDDLES

What has to be broken
before you can use it?
An egg.

What begins with an "e"
but has only one letter?
An envelope.

George's parents
have four children—
Eeny, Meeny, Miny,
and . . . who?
George.

You bought me for
dinner, but never eat
me. What am I?
Utensils.

If you're running in a
race and you pass the
person in second place,
what place are you in?
Second place.

What has a neck but
can't swallow?
A bottle.

What has three feet
but cannot walk?
A yardstick.

What has holes, but
still holds water?
A sponge.

What is white when dirty
and black when clean?
A chalkboard.

What's bigger when
it's upside down?
The number 6.

What bet can
never be won?
The alphabet.

**I'm tall when I'm young, and short
when I'm old. What am I?**

A candle.

What is always served, but cannot be eaten?
A volleyball.

What is so fragile that speaking its name breaks it?
Silence.

What five-letter word becomes shorter when you add two letters to it?
Short.

What occurs once in a minute, twice in a moment, and never in a century?
The letter "m."

What do you feed to give it life, but give it a drink and it dies?
A fire.

What never asks questions but is often answered?
A knock on the door.

What is light as a feather, but even the strongest person in the world can't hold it for more than five minutes?
Your breath.

What is hard as a rock, but disappears in the sun?
An ice cube.

What has keys but no doors, space but no rooms, and you can enter but never leave?
A keyboard.

ANSWER
MASTER RIDDLE

A doctor and a teacher love the same girl. The doctor gave her a rose every day, but the teacher gave her an apple every day. Why did the teacher give her an apple every day?

Because an apple a day keeps the doctor away.

Mike is an editor at BuzzFeed and **Heather** writes the popular parenting website, The Spohrs Are Multiplying. Together, they wrote the book *The Toddler Survival Guide: Complete Protection from the Whiny Unfed*. They live in the greater Los Angeles area with their kids, Annabel and James, and their dog, Schuyler.